The Laws Of Yale College, In New Haven, In Connecticut: Enacted By The President And Fellows

Yale College

In the interest of creating a more extensive selection of rare historical book reprints, we have chosen to reproduce this title even though it may possibly have occasional imperfections such as missing and blurred pages, missing text, poor pictures, markings, dark backgrounds and other reproduction issues beyond our control. Because this work is culturally important, we have made it available as a part of our commitment to protecting, preserving and promoting the world's literature. Thank you for your understanding.

THE

LAWS

OF

YALE-COLLEGE,

IN

NEW-HAVEN,

IN

CONNECTICUT:

ENACTED BY THE

PRESIDENT AND FELLOWS.

NEW-HAVEN:
PRINTED BY WALTER AND STEELE.

1811.

THE
Laws of Yale-College.

CHAPTER I.

Of the Government of the College.

I. THE Government of the College shall be vested in the President, Professors and Tutors, duly elected, qualified and introduced into office, according to the rules established by the Corporation, and shall be styled the Faculty of the College.

II. The President shall have power to direct in all matters relating to the College; to govern the undergraduate Students, and the resident Graduates, and to punish all crimes and offences, committed by them against the laws of the College, except in cases referred by law to the Faculty.

III. The Professors and Tutors, severally, shall have power to govern the undergraduate Students, and to punish them for any crime, except in cases referred by law to the Faculty: Provided that they may not, in any case, proceed contrary to the advice and direction of the President.

IV. The President, at his discretion, shall have authority to appoint a meeting of the Faculty. All matters, which by law are referred to the Faculty, shall be brought before such meetings, and determined by the major part of the members present, whereof the President shall be always one, and concurring in such determination: And when the members present shall be equally divided, the President shall have a casting vote. The Professor of Divinity, whenever he thinks proper, may be excused from attending such meetings, when appointed for the determination of any matter of college discipline and punishment. And in all other cases it shall be the duty of the Professors and Tutors, when requested by the President, to give their opinion and advice.

V. Every judgment for expulsion, dismission for fault, rustication, suspension, public admonition, the second admonition specified in the twenty-third section of the eighth chapter, and sending a student home, shall be by the Faculty; and every judgment for expulsion, dismission and rustication, shall be in writing, and published in such manner as the President shall direct. Copies of all such judgments, on application to the President, shall be given to all persons concerned: And if any Student shall apprehend himself aggrieved by any such judgment, he shall have liberty, at any time within thirty days after the same shall have been given, of applying to the President, by a petition in writing, for a new trial: And on such petition, the President shall, within a convenient time, order a new trial to be had; and provided on such new trial, the former judgment shall be confirmed, such Student, still apprehending himself aggrieved, or, in case he shall be a minor, his Parent or Guardian, shall have the liberty of bringing a petition to the Corporation for relief; which petition he shall lodge with the President, within thirty days after the said new trial: And the President shall lay the said petition before the Corporation, at their next meeting.

VI. Annually, at the Commencement, shall be appointed a Committee, (which shall consist of not less than three members of the Corporation, whereof the President shall be always one, and the other two, or

more, shall be elected by ballot,) called the Prudential Committee; which shall be authorised and required to appoint a Tutor, Butler, or Inspector of the College, whenever any of those offices become vacant, at any other time, than at a meeting of the Corporation—to order such repairs of the College, and other College buildings and appurtenances, as they shall judge necessary—to audit the accounts of the Treasurer and Steward—to make an annual statement and report of the expenditures of the College, and state of the Treasury, and of the revenues and funds of the College—to examine and adjust all accounts, which any person or persons have with the College, and shall lay before them; and where balances shall be found due to any such persons, to give orders on the Treasurer for the payment of them—to institute, or cause to be instituted, in the name of the Corporation, suits for the recovery and preservation of the College property and interest, whenever it shall be necessary—and to do and manage all other matters and things, whereunto they are or shall be further authorised, or required, by law, or by any special resolve of the Corporation.

VII. The President shall be authorised to appoint the meetings of the Committee; and a major part of the Committee shall have power to act: and when any other members of the Corporation shall be present at meetings of the Committee, they shall have the same power of acting as the members of the Committee, in appointing a Tutor, Butler, or Inspector of the College, and in all matters in which their advice and assistance shall be desired by the Committee.

VIII. In case of the death of the President, it shall be the duty of the Prudential Committee to meet immediately at the College; and to make such regulations, and give such orders and directions, as they shall judge necessary; which the Professors, Tutors and Students shall observe, until there shall be a meeting of the Corporation; which meeting the Committee shall call, as soon as may be convenient.

IX. When any person shall have been elected to, and have accepted the office of a Tutor in the College, he shall continue in office for a term not less than two years, unless he shall be permitted by the Corporation, or by the Prudential Committee, to resign sooner. And when any Tutor shall resign the office, or enter upon it at any other time than the Commencement, his part of the salary, for the year ending at the next Commencement, shall be apportioned to the time of his instruction, exclusive of vacations.

CHAPTER II.

Of Admission into the College.....Of the Distinction of the Classes.....Of resident Graduates.....and of the Manners of the Students.

I. AFTER the first of January, 1813, no person shall be admitted into the Freshman Class till he has completed his fifteenth year; nor to an advanced standing, without a proportional increase of age. Candidates for admission into the College shall be examined, in New-Haven, by the President, or, under his direction, by one or more of the Professors or Tutors; and no one shall be admitted, unless he shall be found able to read, translate and parse Cicero's Select Orations, Virgil, and the Greek Testament, and to write true Latin in prose, and shall also have learned the rules of Vulgar Arithmetic.

II. Every Candidate for admission to an advanced standing, shall be examined by the President, and one or more of the Professors or Tutors; or, under the direction of the President, by two or more of the Professors or Tutors; and no such Candidate shall be admitted to such standing, unless he shall be found fully qualified, in all branches of learning proper for the same. But no one, whether a candidate for an advanced standing, or coming from another College, or having been before dismissed from the College, shall be admitted into the Senior Class, after the end of January vacation.

III. No candidate shall be permitted to attend on the collegiate exercises, until he shall have been regularly examined and approved; nor until he shall have given a satisfactory bond to the Treasurer, for the payment of his term bills.

IV. No candidate for an advanced standing shall be allowed to attend on the exercises of the College, until he shall have paid to the College Treasurer a sum equal to the whole of the tuition money which shall have been paid by others of the class into which he shall be admitted. Any Student, however, who comes recommended from any other College, may be admitted without any pecuniary consideration, to the standing for which he shall be found qualified, on examination as before directed, for the admission of candidates to an advanced standing. When any Student, after a dismission from College, shall be re-admitted, he shall first pay to the College Treasurer, a sum equal to the whole of the tuition money which he should have paid, for the standing to which he is admitted, had he not been dismissed.

V. Every candidate for admission into the College, shall produce satisfactory evidence of a blameless life and conversation.

VI. No Student shall be admitted as a member of this College, from any other College, unless he produce a certificate from the proper authority, that he has been subject to no College censure, except on a hearing, the Prudential Committee shall deem it consistent with the interest of the College to admit him.

VII. The Senior Tutor shall keep a matriculation book, in which shall be registered the names of all Students, who, by their regular behavior, and attention to collegiate duties, for six months at least after their admission, shall exhibit evidence satisfactory to the Faculty, of their unblemished moral character. And if any candidate shall fail of exhibiting such evidence, within a reasonable time, he shall be allowed to attend on the exercises of the College no longer. Each candidate shall be particularly required to exhibit proof that he is not guilty of using profane language. All those who are Students on probation, as well as the regular members who have been matriculated, shall be subject to the laws, penalties and discipline of the College.

VIII. No candidate's name shall be registered, until he shall have subscribed the following engagement:

I, A. B. on condition of being admitted as a Member of Yale College, promise, on my Faith and Honor, to observe all the Laws and Regulations of this College; particularly, that I will faithfully avoid using profane language, gaming, and all indecent, disorderly behavior, and disrespectful conduct to the Faculty of the same: as witness my hand,   A. B.

IX. Every Student, not belonging to the town of New-Haven, shall be placed under the guardianship of a patron, who shall be one of the Faculty of the College, and shall be either chosen by the parent or legal guardian of the Student, or appointed by the President: and no Student shall contract any debt without a written permission from his patron, on penalty of being privately dismissed.

X. Masters and Bachelors of Arts, who shall signify to the President their purpose of residing at the College, or in the city of New-Haven, with a view of pursuing literature under his direction, and under the government of the College, and give a sufficient bond to the President and Fellows for the payment of their term bills, shall be considered as resident Graduates and Students of the College.

XI. The Undergraduate Students shall be divided into four distinct classes. The first year they shall be called Freshmen; the second, Sophomores; the third, Junior Sophisters; and the fourth, Senior Sophisters: And in order to preserve a due subordination among the Students, the classes shall give and receive, in the course of their collegiate life, those tokens of respect and subjection, which from common and approved usage belong to their standing in the College. And, if any Scholar shall not comply with this law, or shall be guilty of any abusive speech or behavior towards his fellow-students, or toward any other person, he may be punished by admonition or otherwise, as the offence may require.

XII. If any Student, during the time of his pupilage, shall contract matrimony, he shall no longer be a member of the College.

CHAPTER III.

Of the Religious Worship and Order of the College....Of the Professor of Divinity....and of Monitors.

I. IT shall be the duty of the Faculty, diligently to inspect and watch over the manners and behavior of the Students, and, in all proper methods, both by example and precept, to recommend to them a virtuous and blameless life, and a diligent attention to the public and private duties of religion.

II. The President, or, in his absence, one of the Professors, or one of the Tutors, shall pray every morning and evening, in the Chapel, and read a chapter, or some suitable portion of Scripture; unless a sermon or some other theological discourse shall be delivered. And every undergraduate Student shall be obliged to attend, unless he can render a sufficient excuse for absence.

III. The President is desired frequently to deliver, in the Chapel, lectures or dissertations on such religious, moral, and other subjects, as he shall judge proper for the instruction of the College; which being publicly appointed, every Student shall attend.

IV. Divine worship shall be publicly solemnized in the College, as a distinct religious society, on the Lord's Days; on days of Thanksgiving and Fasting appointed by public authority, and at such other times as shall be appointed by the President. And every undergraduate Student shall be obliged to be present at every exercise of public worship, on every Lord's Day, and on days of public Fasting and Thanksgiving: And no reason of a Student's absence from public worship shall be received as sufficient, unless, when practicable, previously made known to the President, or a Professor, or a Tutor.

V. The Professor of Divinity shall perform the duties of the ministerial and pastoral office in the College. In the discharge of these duties, both public and private, he shall use his best and most faithful endeavors to preserve the Students from irreligion, error and vice; and to promote piety, virtue and good order in this seat of learning; and it shall be his duty, whenever it is required, to lay before the Corporation, or the Prudential Committee, the religious state of the College, and receive their advice and direction in all matters relating to the business of his office. As a standing rule, it is recommended, that about half his public discourses on the Lord's Day, should be in a theological course of lectures or sermons, founded upon scripture texts, in a systematical order; and that the whole course, comprehending a system of Divinity, should be completed in the term of four years: That the other half should be miscellaneous, on such practical and occasional subjects as he shall judge best suited to the religious and moral state and improvement of the College; and that, unless some special reason require a deviation, a discourse of each kind be delivered every Lord's Day. And it shall be his duty to give, from time to time, such lectures and private instructions to the resident Graduates and Students, as he shall judge may best preserve and promote the religious interests of the College, and tend most effectually to form for future usefulness in the work of the evangelical ministry, such of the Students as shall appear desirous of being prepared for it.

VI. It is enjoined upon all the Students to observe the Lord's Day as holy and sacred to the duties of religion: and if any Student shall profane the said day by unnecessary business, by diversion, or by walking abroad, or shall be absent from his chamber on this day, or the preceding evening, or shall thereon admit any other Student or a stranger into his chamber; or on the preceding or following evening shall make indecent noise or disturbance, or shall behave indecently or profanely at the time of public worship, or at prayers, in the Chapel; he may be punished by admonition or otherwise, as the nature and demerit of the crime shall require.

VII. Resident Graduates are required to attend prayers, lectures, and all other exercises of divine worship in the Chapel, under penalty of being deprived of the privilege of the Library for neglect: and if they shall persist in the neglect, or set examples of open profaneness and disregard to the Lord's Day, and the religious order of the College, and after admonition by the President, shall not reform, they shall be adjudged and declared to be no longer resident Graduates, or members of the College, nor allowed to reside in it.

VIII. Monitors shall be appointed by the President, who shall be furnished with bills, in which they shall note down those who are absent from, come late to, or egress from, prayers and other public exercises in the Chapel, on which the Students are by law obliged to attend; which bills they shall deliver to the President, a Professor, or a Tutor, whenever they shall be required.

LAWS OF

CHAPTER IV.

Of the Course of Academic Literature and Instruction in the College.

I. THE Faculty shall instruct the Undergraduate Students in the three learned Languages, the liberal Arts and Sciences, and the whole course of Academic Literature.

II. The Senior Class shall be under the especial instruction of the President: Each Tutor shall take the care of, and instruct the particular Class committed to his charge by the President: The Professors shall deliver public lectures in the Chapel, and private lectures and instructions to the Classes and Students, in the several branches of science which they severally profess, under the direction of the Corporation, or of the Prudential Committee; and where no particular direction is given by the Corporation or the Prudential Committee, under the direction of the President.

III. The President, with the advice of the Professors and Tutors, shall appoint all classical exercises and examinations, and the authors which shall be read and recited by the respective Classes: And it shall be the duty of the President annually at the Commencement to lay before the Corporation the state and method of instruction, the authors recited, and the progress of literary improvement in the College.

Each of the Professors shall, at his discretion, deliver, occasionally, public Lectures in the Chapel.

The Lectures of the Professors of Law, Mathematics, and Chemistry, shall be delivered to the two elder Classes, separate or together, at the discretion of the Professors.

YALE COLLEGE.

The Lectures of the Professor of Divinity shall be delivered to the Senior Class.

The Students of the Classes specified are required universally to assemble at each Lecture, according to the direction of the Professors; and shall by them be required to account for absence, and any other negligence.

Each Student shall take notes of the several heads of the instruction delivered at each Lecture; and shall be examined by the Professors concerning the knowledge which he has gained from the preceding Lecture.

The Professor of Law shall deliver thirty-six Lectures in two years; and in this number shall include his System; and shall deliver a Lecture once in a fortnight, as nearly as may be.

The Professor of Mathematics shall deliver two Lectures in a week to the Senior Class, and a course of experimental Lectures each year to the Junior Class.

The Professor of Chemistry shall deliver four Lectures in a week, until his course is completed.

The Prudential Committee shall be empowered to make temporary alterations in this system, as convenience may require; to exist, in no instance, longer than till the next ensuing session of the Corporation.

IV. The first year of their standing at the College, the Students shall be instructed in the Learned Languages, Arithmetic, Algebra, Geography, and Roman Antiquities. The study of the Languages shall be continued the two following years. In the second year, they shall also be instructed in the Elements of Chronology and History, English Grammar, Logarithms, Geometry, Plane Trigonometry, Mensuration, Surveying, Navigation, Conic Sections, Dialing, and Spherical Geometry and Trigonometry. In the third year, in Fluxions, Natural Philosophy and Astronomy, Chemistry, and the History of Civil Society. In the fourth year, in Chemistry, Natural Philosophy, Astronomy, Rhetoric, Ethics, Logic, Metaphysics, and Theology. The two Senior Classes shall dispute twice a week, before the President or their Tutors. And on Wednesdays, in the afternoon, the three younger Classes shall declaim in the Chapel, from four to six, in each Class, agreeably to the directions of the Faculty. And each one, whenever required, shall deliver his declamation to the President, or to his Tutor, fairly written, with his name subscribed. The Monitors shall previously notify those who are to declaim; and at the time of declaiming deliver a catalogue of them to the President, Professor or Tutor.

V. The Classes shall not go to their recitation rooms, until after the tolling of the bell for the recitation; and shall leave them immediately after the recitation is ended.

VI. The Students who inhabit the recitation rooms, shall receive, of the respective divisions of the Classes, reciting in them, as a compensation for their trouble, the price of the fuel used in them, when brought into the room, during the winter and spring terms; and ten dollars for each room during the summer terms.

VII. If any Student shall be absent from any lecture, recitation, disputation, or other classical exercise duly appointed, he may be admonished: And every Student, who shall be absent from an examination appointed by the Faculty, shall receive such College punishment as the nature of the offence may require.

VIII. There shall be two public examinations, each year; one on the week preceding May Vacation; and the other on the week preceding the Commencement.

IX. If any Student shall appear, on examination, deficient in those branches of knowledge, which according to the regular course of literature in the College he hath been pursuing, it shall be the duty of the President, or his Tutor, to admonish him of such deficiency, that he may be incited to apply with greater diligence to study: and if, notwithstanding, at the next succeeding public examination, holden after an interval of at least three months, he shall appear so deficient as to be unfit for his standing, and unable with profit and reputation to pursue his studies with his Class, he shall be degraded by the Faculty to the next lower Class, or dismissed from the College.

X. The customary public exhibitions in the Chapel, shall be holden under the direction of the President, at the close of the Winter and Spring Terms. If any Student without permission from the Faculty, shall fail to perform the exercise assigned him, he may be sent home.

XI. On the third Wednesday of July, annually, the Senior-Sophisters shall be examined, under the direction of the Faculty, and other Gentlemen of a liberal education, who may be present, as to their knowledge and proficiency in the learned Languages, and liberal Arts and Sciences: And being found well skilled in them, and the whole course of academic literature, shall be advanced to the standing of Candidates for the degree of Bachelor of Arts; and having made all necessary preparations for Commencement, the President may give them leave of absence from the College, until the Friday before the Commencement.

XII. If any member of the Senior Class absent himself from the July Examination, without reasons satisfactory to the Faculty, he shall be precluded receiving a degree with his Class.

XIII. No candidate shall be permitted to exhibit on the Public Commencement, unless he present his composition for correction, on or before the Monday preceding the July Examination.

CHAPTER V.

Of Vacations, and of Absence from the College.

I. THERE shall be three Vacations annually. The first, six weeks immediately after Commencement: The second, three weeks from the second Wednesday in January: The third, three weeks from the Wednesday immediately preceding the second Thursday in May.

II. The President shall appoint some suitable person, who during the Vacation shall take care of, and prevent damages from being done to the College, or to any of the appurtenances belonging to it. And such person shall have a reasonable compensation made him by the Corporation.

III. No Undergraduate shall reside in the College, during any of the Vacations, without the knowledge and permission of the President: And if any one shall transgress this law, he shall be fined not exceeding twenty cents for each day.

IV. Immediately upon the expiration of every Vacation, the Undergraduate Students shall assemble at the College: If any Student shall voluntarily absent himself from the College without a just and reasonable excuse, when by law he ought to be present, the Faculty shall have power, at their discretion, to correct such disobedience by fine, not exceeding fifty cents by the day, during such absence, or by admonition, or by sending him away from the College, as the nature of the case may require.

CHAPTER VI.

Of the Location of the Students.

I. THE President shall have authority to locate the Students in the chambers and studies of the College; and if any Student shall refuse to dwell in the chamber assigned to him by the President, he shall be dismissed from the College: and if any Student shall remove from his own into an other chamber; or make up his bed for lodging in any other chamber than his own, he may be fined or punished in some other way, as the circumstances of the case may require.

II. If any Student to whom a chamber is assigned, shall be absent from the College beyond the time allowed him, or shall be vexatious to his chamber mates, or shall injure the chamber, or there shall be any other sufficient cause, the President may, at his discretion, take away a chamber from him to whom it is assigned, and dispose of it to another.

III. Each Tutor, either personally or by exchange, shall, so far as may be convenient, visit the several rooms bordering on the entry in which he resides, once or twice a day.

IV. No Student shall walk abroad, or be absent from his chamber, (except to attend the collegiate exercises) in the hours of study, which shall be, from the tolling of the study bell, in the morning and afternoon, till the close of the succeeding recitations.

V. Every Student, whether present or absent, shall be at the expence of his proportion of furniture, wood and candles, necessary for the chamber assigned to him.

VI. If the College chambers shall not be sufficient to receive all the Students, the President shall give liberty to so many as necessity shall require, to reside among the inhabitants of New-Haven, of a good and approved character: In which case a preference shall be allowed to such Students as belong to the city, when it shall be requested by them, their parents or guardians, that they may reside in the families to which they belong. If any other Student shall fix his residence in any house in the city, or remove from one house to another without the previous knowledge and allowance of the President, he shall be fined not exceeding thirty-six cents; and six cents for every day, during which he shall continue to reside in any such house without making it known to the President. And if, after the express disallowance of the President, any Student shall fix or continue his residence in any house in the city, he shall be dismissed from the College.

VII. All Students living out of the College, and in the town of New-Haven, shall be subject to the same laws and rules in their chambers, as those who reside in the College.

CHAPTER VII.

Of College Damages, and the Assessment of them.

I. WHEN any damage shall be found done, except by the inevitable Providence of God, to any chamber or study in the College, the person or persons to whom such chamber or study is assigned and belongs, shall make good the same, unless such damage shall have happened while they were absent, in Vacation. And when any damage is done to any chamber or study in Vacation, or to any other parts of the College, or the appurtenances thereof at any time, the same shall be assessed upon all the Undergraduate Students, and charged in their quarter-bills: Provided always, if the person or persons who were principals or accessories in doing any such damages, shall be discovered, he or they shall make full satisfaction for the same; and if they shall have been done intentionally by any Student or Students, they shall each be liable to a fine not exceeding three dollars and thirty-three cents, and to any other College punishment which the circumstances of the offence shall require.

II. The President shall cause to be estimated all damages of broken glass at the end of every term, and the same to be assessed upon the Students according to law, and charged in their terms bills.

III. To ascertain other damages done to the College buildings and appurtenances, there shall be annually appointed at Commencement three persons, who shall be called Inspectors of the College, and any two of them have power to act; whose duty it shall be to inspect and estimate all damages done to the College, buildings and appurtenances, whenever they shall be required by the President: They shall also, *ex officio*, inspect and set down in writing, the state of every chamber, and study at the beginning and ending of every Vacation, and likewise of the buildings and appurtenances of the College; and at the end of each term and of each Vacation, they shall estimate the damages done to each chamber and study, or to other parts of the College buildings and appurtenances during the preceding term or Vacation, which had not before been estimated, on the special request of the President. And all estimates of damages, particularly stated, the Inspectors shall deliver to the President in writing, with their names subscribed; which estimates, with a reasonable compensation to the Inspectors for their trouble, shall be the rule by which the Undergraduates shall be assessed and charged respectively by the President for damages, in the term bill, next after such estimates shall have been made.

IV. All damages estimated by the Inspectors of the College, shall, by order of the President, be immediately repaired, when practicable; and when in the opinion of the Inspectors it shall be expedient, that any damage done to the College, or to any of the appurtenances thereof, should be repaired before an estimate of such damage is made, the President shall order the repair to be made; and provided the repair is full and complete, the actual expence shall be a rule to the Inspectors in the estimate of the damage; otherwise it shall be assessed according to their discretion.

V. No repairs, additions or alterations shall be made in any chamber of the College, or in the appurtenances of any chamber, by any Student or Students, but at his or their own expence, and under the direction of the Inspectors of the College, on penalty of a fine not exceeding three dollars and sixty-seven cents for each offence.

VI. Whenever in the opinion of the Inspectors of the College it shall be necessary that the chapel, or any of the public chambers or entries of the College, or the chambers of the Students, or any of them, should be whitewashed, the same shall be done by order of the President, under the direction of the Inspectors, or some one of them; the expence of which shall be paid out of the College Treasury.

VII. The Inspectors of the College shall be authorised to judge and determine whether the College chambers are fit for the reception of the Students; and if on inspection of any chamber, it is not in their opinion fit to be inhabited, no Student shall be obliged to reside in such chamber, until it shall be repaired, and judged by the Inspectors fit to be inhabited.

CHAPTER VIII.

Of Crimes and Misdemeanors.

I. Every Student, whether a Graduate or Undergraduate, shall be subject to the laws and government of the College, and shew, in speech and behavior, all proper tokens of reverence and obedience to the Faculty of the College: And if any Student shall transgress this law, by treating them, or any of them, with reviling or reproachful language; or by behaving contumaciously or contemptuously toward them, or by being guilty of any kind of contempt of their persons or authority, he may be punished by any censure, even to expulsion, as the nature and aggravations of his crime may require.

II. If any Student shall deny the Holy Scriptures, or any part thereof, to be of divine authority; or shall assert and endeavor to propagate among the Students any error or heresy, subverting the foundation of the Christian religion, and shall persist therein after admonition, he shall be dismissed.

III. If any Student shall be guilty of blasphemy, robbery, fornication, theft, forgery, duelling, or any other crime, for which an infamous punishment may be inflicted by the laws of the State, he shall be expelled.

IV. If any Student shall assault, wound, or strike the President, a Professor, or a Tutor, or shall maliciously or designedly break their windows or doors, he shall be expelled.

V. If any Student shall be guilty of fighting, striking, quarrelling, challenging, turbulent words or behavior, wearing women's apparel, fraud, lying, defamation, or any such like crimes, he shall be punished by fine, admonition, or other College punishment, suited to the nature and demerit of the crime.

VI. If any Student shall break open the door of another; or privately pick his lock with any instrument, for the first offence he shall be fined eighty cents; and for the second, fined, admonished or expelled, as the nature of the offence may deserve.

VII. If any Student shall be guilty of an injury to a fellow-student, or to any other person within the town of New-Haven, upon complaint and proof thereof made to the President, he shall, with the advice of the Professors and Tutors, give judgment thereon, and order satisfaction to be made according to the nature of the offence or injury; which if any Student refuse to do, he shall be publicly admonished; and if, after admonition, he persist in such refusal, he shall be dismissed.

VIII. The President, a Professor or a Tutor, shall have authority to break open and enter any College chamber or study, at all times at discretion. And if any Student shall refuse to admit the President, or any one of the Professors or of the Tutors into his chamber or study; or to assist them in suppressing any disorder, or to give his evidence respecting any matter under examination, when in any of those cases required; or shall falsely declare himself ignorant of the matter, he may be punished by admonition, suspension, rustication, or expulsion, as the circumstances of the crime may require.

IX. If any Student shall undress himself for swimming in any place, exposed to public view, he may be punished, as the circumstances may require.

X. If any Student without leave obtained of the President, or one of the Professors, or of the Tutors, shall go out of the town of New-Haven, or beyond the place allowed him, or shall not return by the appointed time, he may be punished by fine, admonition or otherwise, according to the degree and circumstances of the offence.

XI. No Student shall go a sailing without permission first obtained of the President.

XII. If any Student shall play at hand or foot-ball in the College-yard, or throw any thing against the College-building, or fence, by which they may be in danger of damage, he shall be fined eight cents.

XIII. Every Student in studying time, shall abstain from hallooing, singing, loud talking, playing on a musical instrument, and other noise in the College, or College yard.

XIV. If any Student shall ring the College-bell, except by order of the President, a Professor, Tutor or the Butler, shall be fined, or otherwise punished, as the case may require.

XV. If any student shall keep any kind of fire-arms or gun-powder, or shall fire any gun-powder in or near the College-yard, or near the dwelling-house or the person of the President, a Professor or a Tutor, he shall be admonished, rusticated, or otherwise punished as the case may require.

XVI. If any Student shall, any where in New-Haven, act a part in, or be present at the acting of any comedy or tragedy, he shall be fined not exceeding eighty cents.

XVII. If any Student shall attend any dancing assembly, or dancing school in the City of New-Haven, in term time, he may be admonished, suspended or sent home.

XVIII. If any Student shall play at billiards, cards or dice, or any other unlawful game, or at back gammon, or at any game for a wager; or shall keep in his chamber, cards, or a back gammon board; or shall call for any strong drink in any tavern or other place within two miles of the College, he shall be punished for the first offence by admonition, and for any subsequent offence may be rusticated, suspended or sent home.

XIX. If any Student shall venture money or goods in any kind of lottery, or chance game, not allowed by the laws of the land, he shall be punished by admonition, rustication or expulsion, as the nature and circumstances of the case may require.

XX. If any person not belonging to the College shall contemptuously treat or abuse the Faculty of the College; or shall instigate, advise or aid any Student to a refractory and stubborn behavior or carriage towards the Laws and Governors of the College; or shall draw away or seduce any of the Students into vile principles or practices, the President, a Professor or Tutor, may forbid the person so offending to enter into the College-yard, and also prohibit the Students to hold any intercourse with him, which if any Student shall have, after such prohibition, he may be admonished or otherwise punished at the discretion of the Faculty.

XXI. If any combination or agreement to do any unlawful act, or to forbear compliance with any injunction from lawful authority in the College, shall be entered into by Undergraduates; or if any enormity, disorder, or act of disobedience shall be perpetrated by any

Undergraduates in consequence of such combination or agreement, in both or either of those cases, such and so many of the offenders, shall, upon due conviction, be punished with admonition, rustication, dismission or expulsion according to the circumstances of their offences, as shall be judged necessary for the preservation of good order in the College.

XXII. In all cases when an offence is committed frequently or daringly, the Faculty shall have power to enhance the punishment at their discretion: In all cases the Faculty may accept an ingenuous public confession, in lieu of a penalty, except where the law requires expulsion.

XXIII. Whenever any member of the College Faculty shall be satisfied that any Student is guilty of frequent absence from prayers, public worship, or any College exercises, established by law; or of disorderly behavior, when present at any of them, or in the dining hall; or of unreasonable expensiveness in living or apparel, or improper company keeping, in his room, or elsewhere; or of idleness, or profane language, or profaning the Sabbath; or that he has gone out of College limits without leave, or has attended a dancing-school, or dancing assemblies; or procured, or received meals, or other entertainment, in any Tavern or boarding-house; or frequented such house or houses; or that he absents himself from his room, after 10 o'clock at night; or is frequently absent from his room in study hours; or has been guilty of any loose conduct, or of disrespectful behavior to any officer of this College; he shall be admonished of his misbehavior by his Instructor, or any other Member of the Faculty; and, if he continue unreformed, it shall be notified to the Faculty, who shall admonish him again, and make known his case to his Parent or Guardian; if he continue still unreformed, he shall be sent home; and shall never be readmitted, except by a major vote of the Faculty.

XXIV. Every Student shall be answerable for all vicious, scandalous, and immoral conduct, during the several Vacations, in the same manner as in term time.

XXV. No Student shall be questioned for any testimony he may give in regard to a violation of a law of this College; and in case any Student shall so question his fellow Student to ascertain whether he hath testified, or with intent to bring him into contempt; or shall endeavor to bring into contempt any Student, because he has testified, the Student so acting, shall be deemed to have committed an offence; and may be proceeded against by the Faculty, according to the aggravation of the offence, even to dismission.

XXVI. Whereas the Laws of the College are few and general, and cases may occur which are not expressly provided for by law: in all such cases, the Faculty shall proceed according to their best discretion, and may punish a Student by inflicting any College censure, according to the nature and circumstances of his crime.

XXVII. The President shall cause a bill of the fines and other punishments, inflicted upon the Students for misdemeanors and crimes, to be kept for the inspection of their parents and guardians, whenever they shall request it; which bill shall contain a summary account of the reasons of such fines and punishments.

CHAPTER IX.

Of the Library....Of the Museum....Of the Philosophical Chamber and Apparatus.

I. NO person, except the President, Fellows, Members of the Faculty, resident Graduates, and Senior and Junior Sophisters, shall have the liberty of drawing books out of the Library, but by permission from the President and Professors. No book shall be borrowed from the Library, except by the President, without the knowledge and presence of the Librarian; and no person but the Librarian, except the President, shall have a key to the Library.

II. The Library shall be opened on Thursday of each week, Vacations excepted, between the hours of two and three in the afternoon. No Student shall be allowed to draw books from the Library oftener than once in a fortnight; and the Senior and Junior classes shall have, in their order, their distinct weeks for drawing.— Graduates may attend the Library every Thursday, at the time above specified. But the Librarian shall be obliged to wait on any of the gentlemen in the government and instruction of the College, whenever they shall have occasion to go into the Library.

No persons, except members of the Faculty, may have more than three books out at a time.

III. The President shall register such books as he shall take from the Library, and the Librarian shall register all other books which shall be borrowed from the Library, noting the title and size of the books, the name of the borrower, the time when borrowed, and when returned. No person shall lend to another a book which he has borrowed from the Library, nor let it go from his possession; and no Student, Graduate or Undergraduate, shall carry a book belonging to the Library out of the city of New-Haven, on penalty, in each of the cases aforesaid, of being deprived of the privilege of borrowing books for a time not exceeding six months, or of paying a fine not exceeding one dollar, at the discretion of the Faculty.

IV. Such of the books, as being of great value are proper to be consulted only occasionally, and shall be designated by the Corporation, or in their recess by the Prudential Committee, with the aid of the Faculty, shall not be taken out of the Library, excepting only by the Faculty.

V. Resident Graduates and Undergraduates, and such persons as have special licence to borrow books from the Library, shall pay to the Librarian at the rate of twelve cents every month, for a Folio Volume, eight vol. cents for a Quarto, six cents for an Octavo, or lesser volume; and double the sum for every book that is recited; and if the book be not returned within a month from the time when it was borrowed, double the sum shall be paid, every month, until it shall be returned. If the book be not returned within six months, the person who detains it shall be liable to pay double the value of the same; and if it belongs to a set of books, to double the value of the set. And whosoever shall borrow a book from the Library, shall make good all damages done to it while in his possession, at the discretion of the President or the Librarian.

VI. No candidate shall be admitted to a degree until he shall have produced a certificate from the Librarian, that he has returned all the books which he has borrowed from the Library.

VII. The Philosophical Chamber, the Apparatus Room, and Apparatus shall be under the care of the Professor of Mathematics and Natural Philosophy.

VIII. No person, except the President, or some other officer in the government of the College, or by permission of the President, or of such other officer, shall be allowed to go into the Museum, the Philosophical Chamber, or Apparatus Room, without the Professor of the Mathematics and Natural Philosophy, who shall take care that the several instruments, machines and other articles, deposited in them, be in their proper places, and in good order, and make report of their state to the Corporation, whenever he shall find it necessary, or shall be required.

CHAPTER X.

Of the Butler.

I. THE Butler shall employ a proper person to attend in the Buttery, who, at the hour of prayer, shall wait on the President, or in his absence, on one of the Professors or Tutors; and having received his orders, shall ring the bell; on which the Students shall assemble in the Chapel. In like manner, he shall wait on the President, or on one of the Professors and Tutors, and by their direction shall ring the bell for all public meetings, lectures, and other occasions, attend in the Chapel by the President's appointment, for study and recitation; and at all other times, when required by the President, a Professor, or a Tutor.

II. The Butler shall be allowed to sell, in the Buttery, Cider, Metheglin, small and strong Beer, and such other articles, as the President shall judge necessary for the Students, and permit in writing: But no permission shall be granted for selling wine or distilled spirits; and no Student shall be allowed by the Butler at any time to use or consume any article in the room which hath been bought there. The Butler shall observe the orders of the President in all things relating to the Buttery, and whenever required, shall shew him all articles which he hath for sale, and his accounts with the Students, and no charge except for permitted articles shall be allowed in his quarter-bill.

III. The Butler shall not sell any other than permitted articles for ready money to any Student, nor allow any Student to contract a debt at the Buttery exceeding one dollar twenty-five cents per month, except for Books to be recited, unless such Student be of age; or his parent or guardian signify to the Butler in writing, that a larger credit be given him; in which case the Butler may go on to credit such Student to the amount of two dollars fifty cents per month, and no further.

IV. The Butler, as a compensation for his expence, shall be allowed a reasonable advance on the net cost of the articles sold by him under the direction of the President. And, at the close of each quarter, the Butler shall make up his bill against each Student, in which every article sized or taken up by him at the Buttery, shall be particularly charged, which bill shall be subject to the correction of the President, and being approved and signed by him, the Students shall be obliged to pay the same; and if not paid within one month, interest till paid.

V. For the privilege of the Buttery, the Butler shall provide candles, and light them in the Chapel, at prayers and on other occasions at his own expence, unless it shall be otherwise ordered by the Corporation.

VI. The Butler shall be removable from his office for misbehaviour by the Corporation, or in their absence by the Prudential Committee, at their discretion.

CHAPTER XI.

Of Commons.

I. THE Steward appointed by the Corporation shall, when required by the President, provide in the College Hall, victuals, after the manner of living in common families, for all the Professors and Tutors, Graduates and Undergraduates, who reside in the College; and shall at all times cause the tables to be decently spread and attended, at such a price as shall be fixed by the Corporation. And if any Student residing in the College refuse to be in Commons, he shall be dismissed from the College.

II. No graduate residing in College shall put himself out of Commons, but with the leave of the President; and no Undergraduate shall be put out of Commons, without a written order from the President, or one of the Professors or Tutors: Nor shall any such leave, or order, be granted to any Graduate or Undergraduate, residing in the College, saving only in case of sickness, unless he properly belong to some family in the city of New-Haven, in which case he may be permitted to receive his diet in such family, when requested, and no other. The Prudential Committee, however, shall be authorised to grant an exemption from being in Commons to any Student, for other reasons than of sickness, when they shall appear sufficiently great and urgent to justify the same.

III. At every meal, one of the Tutors, or Graduates, or in their absence, a Senior Sophister shall ask a blessing on the food, and return thanks:—And all the Scholars shall at meal times behave themselves decently, abstaining from all rude and loud talking, and keeping in their places until thanks shall have been returned. No kitchen furniture or utensils shall be carried out of the Hall; nor any victuals to any Undergraduate, unless in case of sickness, or for other good reason, and by an order from the President, a Professor, or a Tutor: If any Student transgress in either of these things, he shall be fined or otherwise punished, according to the circumstances and aggravations of the offence.

IV. The Students shall not assemble, before or in the Hall or Kitchen, in the interval between the ringing and tolling of the bell for their meal.

V. Waiters shall be appointed by the President, who shall attend the tables in the Hall at every meal; for which a reasonable compensation shall be made them by the Steward. If any waiter, before the end of the year, for which he was appointed, shall cease to wait; without leave first obtained of the President, he shall forfeit his compensation for the preceding part of the year. The waiters, before they leave the Hall, after each meal, shall make a return in writing to the Steward of all damages done to the utensils at said meal, and of the names of the persons who did the same, if known; and shall see that all utensils delivered into the Hall be returned back into the kitchen. If the waiters neglect to comply with this law, they shall be accountable to the Steward, and charged in their term bills for all damages sustained through such neglect. The Steward shall keep an account of all damages notified by the waiters, and all other damages and loss of utensils, and the same exhibit every term to the Prudential Committee, who shall assess such damages and losses, unless such as happened through his default, or the default of his servants in the kitchen, and charge the same in the Steward's next term bill, to the persons by whom they were done, or through whose neglect or default they happened, if known; otherwise to all the students who were in Commons at the time, or during the quarter when they were done or happened.

VI. If any Undergraduate, when in Commons, shall breakfast, dine or sup, except gratis upon invitation, in any house in the city, or shall procure such meal to be brought to him from the town, in either case, unless he had previous leave from the President, a Professor, or a Tutor, he shall be admonished.

CHAPTER XII.

Of College Dues and Quarter Bills.

I. The bills of the Students of this College shall be made up three times each year; the first on the second Wednesday of January; the second on the second Wednesday of May; and the third on the second Wednesday of September. Every Student shall be charged for tuition eleven dollars each term; for study rent two dollars; for ordinary repairs and other contingent charges, eighty cents; for sweeping, living out of the College, eight cents; for sweeping and making beds, living in the College, forty-four cents; excepting that the graduated Students shall be exempted from tuition and contingent charges; together with the sums assessed during the quarter for broken glass, for other damages, for fines, for expence of classical catalogues, and other customary College dues: Likewise in the bill of the term ending at Commencement, the candidates for the first degree shall be charged with the sum of one dollar for the triennial printing of the College Catalogue, and with the sum of two dollars for the expence of the public Commencement dinner, unless said sums shall be otherwise stated by the Corporation. The candidates for the second degree shall pay a like sum to the Treasurer for the public dinner, or to the Scribe of the Corporation, who shall deliver the same to the Treasurer. The President, having approved and signed the said bills, shall deliver one of them to the Treasurer of the College, and keep the other himself; and thereon take a writing signed by the Treasurer, acknowledging his receipt of the other bill, and that he will be accountable to the President and Fellows for the whole sum therein contained: And the Treasurer shall collect the same of the Students, and shall pay three times a year to the officers of the College the sums due to them, charging said sums to the Corporation, with all other sums paid by their order, or by order of the Prudential Committee, and likewise pay three times a year to the Sweeper of the College such a sum as by agreement of the Corporation or of the Prudential Committee, shall have become his due; the same being certified by the President.

II. The usual expences, incurred in preparations for, and attending Commencement, which have been heretofore defrayed by the Class, which have been graduated as Bachelors, shall be contracted hereafter, under the direction of the Steward; and to defray the same the individuals of the Class to be graduated shall be charged one dollar each in the term bill, for the term ending at Commencement, and collected as other dues are collected.

III. In like manner, towards the end of each term, the Steward shall write a bill of the several sums payable to him for Commons at the price stated by the President and Fellows, with a duplicate thereof, both which bills he shall present to the President; and the President, having approved and signed them, shall deliver one of them to the Steward and keep the other himself, and thereon take a writing signed by the Steward, acknowledging the receipt of the other bill, which he shall be authorised to collect of the Students, and apply to his own use; and if he shall not be able to collect the sums of money due on said bill without a suit, he shall have a right to use the bond given to the President and Fellows, provided he shall give sufficient security to the Treasurer to indemnify them.

IV. All the Students in the College shall pay their respective shares of the Steward's salary.

V. The several sums charged in the term bills, shall be considered as due and payable as soon as the bills are made up according to law; and the Treasurer shall be authorised to demand the same, immediately on the bill's being delivered to him for collection, with interest for all the time afterwards, during which they shall remain unpaid. Provided that no Student who shall pay his term bills within a fortnight after the end of the Vacation, immediately following the date of said bill, shall be charged interest on the same.

VI. At the close of each term a bill shall be delivered to each Student, containing the charges of the Treasurer and the Steward against him for the preceding term; and each Student shall be required to exhibit said bill to his parent, guardian, or patron.

If any Student do not pay his term bill, as has been expressed, he shall, on his return to College at the close of the Vacation, exhibit to the Treasurer a certificate, signed by his parent, guardian or patron, of the delivery to him of said bill. And, in case any Student shall neglect to exhibit said certificate to the Treasurer, he shall not be permitted to recite, until such exhibition shall be made, unless he shall render a reason, satisfactory to the Faculty.

VII. If any Student shall neglect to pay within fourteen days after the close of any Vacation, his bills of the preceding term, both to the Treasurer and Steward, he shall thereafter be charged for tuition, ten cents a week over and above the stated rate of tuition, for such time as either of said bills shall remain unpaid. Provided, that Students who shall not return within fourteen days after the close of any Vacation, shall not be chargeable with additional tuition, till the expiration of five days after their return; provided also, that the President may, for sufficient reasons, grant to any Student exemption from additional tuition, until the next meeting of the Prudential Committee; and the Prudential Committee may, in like manner, grant exemption for such time as they may think reasonable.

VIII. It shall be the duty of the Monitors to report to the Treasurer, immediately on the expiration of fourteen days, after the close of each Vacation, the names of all such Students as have not returned to College; and upon the return of any Student who has been reported as absent, the Monitor of such Student's Class, shall give notice to the Treasurer of his return.

IX. In case of the absence, sickness, or any other incapacity of the President, and also in case the President's office shall be vacant, the senior Tutor at the College shall be authorised and required to do every thing relating to the quarter bills of the Treasurer, Steward and Butler, which by law the President is authorised and required to do.

X. The Treasurer shall report to the President at the beginning of each term, such Students as have not given bonds.

XI. No Student shall board in any public inn or tavern in New-Haven.

CHAPTER XIII.

Of Commencement and Academical Degrees.

I. THE Commencement shall be on the second Wednesday of September annually, and the Candidates for the first degree shall attend at the College, on the Friday preceding.

II. No Student may expect the honor of the first degree, who hath not attended and performed the course of academical exercises, as appointed by law for the space of four years; except such as have been regularly admitted to an advanced standing; nor unless on the examination in July, or a special examination appointed by the President, he shall have been approved as a candidate for the same; and also have, on the day before the Commencement, produced certificates from the Treasurer, the Butler, and the Librarian, that he has paid to them their respective dues.

III. No Candidate for the second degree may expect the honor of the same, unless he shall have preserved a good moral character, and previously to the Commencement signified to the President his desire of the same: All Candidates for either degree shall be personally present, unless in any instance the President and Fellows shall judge it proper to confer the honor of a degree upon an absent Candidate, in which case he shall pay into the College Treasury one dollar, or such greater sum as the President and Fellows shall appoint. And certificates from the Treasurer, that the money required of the Candidates for the second degree, for the public dinner, and likewise of absent Candidates, has been paid to him, shall be produced to the Scribe of the Corporation on the Commencement morning; or said money may be paid to the Scribe, who shall be accountable to the Treasurer for the same, or so much thereof as he shall receive.

IV. All academical honors shall be given by the President, with the consent of the Fellows; and the Candidates for a first or a second degree, shall, each, for the same, pay to the President four dollars.

V. The Candidates for either degree shall attend the public procession on the Commencement day, from and to the College: and shall perform the public exercises, which shall have been previously appointed for them by the President; and no public exhibition shall be made without such appointment, nor without having been approved by the President. And if any Student, without permission from the Faculty, shall fail to perform the exercise which has been allotted to him; or shall speak any thing which has not been approved by the Faculty, he may be deprived of a degree. The President shall begin and close the business and public entertainments of the day with prayer.

VI. There shall be no parade, illumination or fire works at the time of the Commencement, but by the permission and under the direction of the President: and if any Candidate for a degree, or any Student shall transgress this law, he shall be punished by the President and Fellows at their discretion.

VII. No Student who shall receive any appointment to exhibit before the Class, the College, or the Public, shall give any treat of wine or spirituous liquors to his Class, or any part thereof, for, or on account of those appointments, or under color thereof, on penalty of admonition, rustication, or of being denied the honors of the College, as to the Faculty shall seem just and necessary, and proportioned to the nature of the offence.

Printed by Libri Plureos GmbH in Hamburg, Germany